Sally and the Rock-wallabies

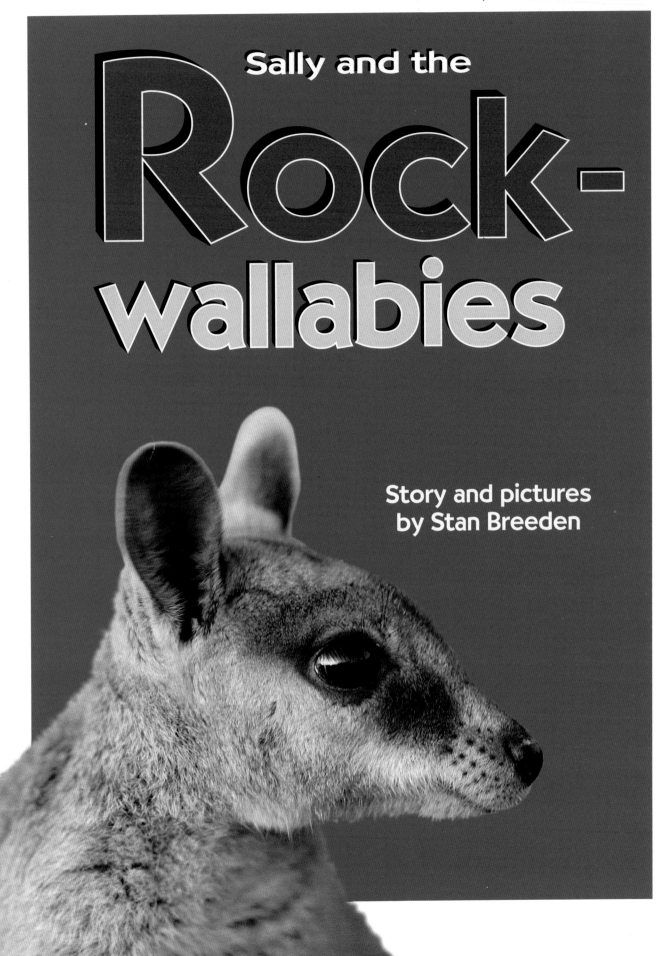

Story and pictures
by Stan Breeden

Sally loves the woodlands near her home in the tropics. Here there are long grasses, shrubby trees - and wonderful rock formations.

In summer the woodlands are very hot, so she prefers to explore in the spring. Early mornings are best, when birds sing and flowers are fresh. If she is very still, interesting things can happen. Sometimes, an agile wallaby hops by, or one with a large young in her pouch stops to look at Sally.

Sally often wishes that she could find a special place, somewhere magical. She loves to read about places like that.

One day, as she leans against an ironbark tree day-dreaming, she hears a very strange sound....

The sound comes from bushes growing beside a flat rock - "djoow djoow". It is like a whistle. Then it changes to a kind of rasping wheeze - "djoowee, djoowee". Suddenly, the sound changes again, to hissing and rattling. Sally creeps closer and peers around a bush. She is amazed by what she sees.

A bird is singing and dancing around two piles of small objects. Most are white, but some are green, silver or red. There are hundreds of them. Between the piles stand two rows of fine twigs forming a kind of archway.

The great bowerbird – for that is the bird's name – picks up some of his ornaments, one after another, and rearranges them. Soon he flies off. This is truly magical, Sally thinks.

Sally walks over to the bird's bower to examine it more closely. There are white snail shells and bones, but also pieces of glass – some green, some clear - silver paper, small pieces of aluminium, lots of red plastic and even a few green fruit.

Sally can hear another unexpected sound in this dry country. Faintly in the distance, she hears a creek running. She goes off to explore. After seeing such a magical bird, what else might she discover?

Sally walks on through the woodlands and up a rocky hill.

She stops, spellbound at what she sees below her.

There is a deep ravine. Rocks and boulders, some taller than a house, lie tumbled together. Strange formations, like castles, are reflected in pools of quiet water. Giant fig trees cling to the rocks and there are patches of greener grass where flowers grow. She hears the songs of different kinds of birds. Beyond the ravine, as far as Sally can see, are more rocks.

Hopping from rock to rock, Sally goes down into the ravine. At the bottom she sits quietly, just looking. The rocks are very rough and dark with lichens growing on them in many places.

Slowly Sally realises that some of the small rocks are not rough, but soft. They have ears and tails and move about. Many pairs of bright eyes watch her. On top of a high boulder she sees the shape of a small wallaby - only for a moment - then it is gone.

Another jumps across a chasm. It is just a blur. About ten rock-wallabies, sitting on ledges and in small caves, look down at Sally.

So quiet and still is Sally that the rock-wallabies seem to forget about her. But they remain alert and do not come too close. Only one relaxes. It sits on its rump with its long tail folded forwards. Sally creeps away quietly to look for the creek.

She can hear water running quite clearly now.

Sally climbs down further and further. When she finds the creek, she spreads her arms wide in delight.

The clear, cool creek runs over smooth rocks. There are green plants all around. Weeping bottle brush trees are covered with bright red flowers.

A scarlet honeyeater sips nectar from the flowers and then flies off to the nest to feed his young.

Dragonflies of all colours land on branches or stones, soon to zip off again. From a cool shady spot, a dwarf tree frog calls.

Striped marsh frogs hide among rocks. A skink looks briefly at Sally before dashing off.

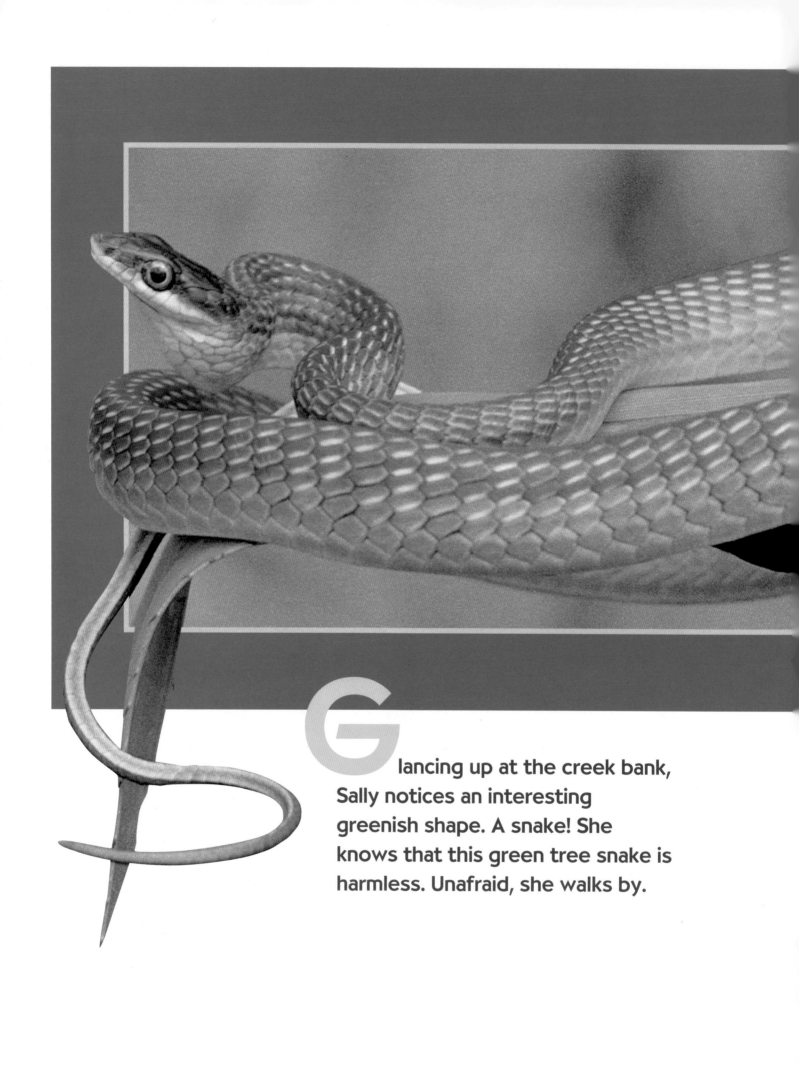

Glancing up at the creek bank, Sally notices an interesting greenish shape. A snake! She knows that this green tree snake is harmless. Unafraid, she walks by.

 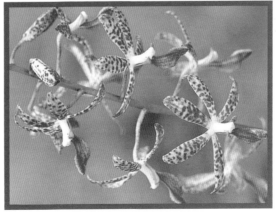

She stops to admire a pink hibiscus flower
and a spray of hyacinth orchids.

As she bends over to sniff the flowers, she spots a squatter pigeon sitting on its nest on the ground. A cedar bush brown butterfly rests on a grass blade.

Above it, two lemon migrant butterflies have just come out of their pupae. A pink striped weevil looks at Sally from a leaf.

Nearby, a jewel beetle eats a flower petal. The more Sally looks the more she sees.

Sally has found her magic place. It is more wonderful than she could ever have imagined. Now she wants to make friends with the rock-wallabies. They make the woodlands really special.

The rock-wallabies are as curious about Sally as she is about them.

Soon they know each other well.

Sally shares the raisins she has in her pocket.

She offers the wallabies grevillea flowers. They love the sweet nectar and eat the whole flower. Sally reaches out and touches one of the little animals. Their fur is very, very soft.

Sally sits among the wallabies for hours and learns about how they live. In the late afternoon, she watches them leave their rocks to find grass to eat.

Sally notices that not all rock-wallabies look the same. They are just like people - each face is slightly different. Rock-wallabies have huge eyes with long lashes.

Rock-wallabies can show great affection for each other. As part of their courtship, a male and a female will groom each other's fur.

Gently, and with obvious enjoyment, one will nibble the other with its teeth.

In the early morning it can be cold among the rocks. The wallabies like to warm themselves in the sun.

They relax and sit on their rumps.

Rock-wallabies clean themselves thoroughly. They lick their paws and rub them over their faces.

They even wash behind their ears. To groom their fur, they scratch with the nails on their paws and the small nails on their feet.

The inside of the pouch, including the young one, is also thoroughly cleaned.

Sally is especially fond of the mothers who have large young ones in their pouches.

Even when the babies are barely covered with fur, they stick their heads out and look around.

When they are completely covered with fur, the young ones lean right out. The pouches stretch so much they seem to be made of elastic. The mothers tip the larger young out so they can clean the insides of their pouches.

The youngsters are easily frightened and try to climb back in as quickly as they can. They have good reason to be frightened.

Sometimes Sally worries about the rock-wallabies.

She watches anxiously when a wedge-tailed eagle lands in a dead tree near the rocks. A young rock-wallaby can be a tasty meal for the eagle. In a flash, it can snatch one right off the rocks with its sharp claws.
In front of a dark cave, Sally surprises a black-headed python, sunning itself.

If a python were to grab one of the wallabies, it would never escape from the snake's tight coils.

But the wallabies are quick. At great speed, they leap up and down and in between the rocks. They seem to bound like soft furry balls. They are nearly always too quick for eagles and pythons.

The wallabies have soft leathery soles on their feet. They never slip when they dash about. Their soles are just like those on Sally's boots.

Sally climbs one of the big fig trees that grow among the rocks. She watches the rock-wallabies from a fork in the trunk.

Above her, many birds eat the ripe figs. Bowerbirds visit. A black-faced cuckoo shrike also eats figs. A pair has a nest close by.

In another tree, a male fig bird sits on its nest incubating the eggs. Once the eggs hatch, both parents will feed the young on insects as well as the colourful fruit.

This is how Sally found her magic place. There may be one near you. Perhaps it is in a gnarled and hollow tree where bats and owls live. Maybe it is a beach where giant turtles come to lay their eggs. It might be a damp dark rainforest, green with moss and ferns, where lyrebirds dance.

There are wild and magic places everywhere.